C Major Shifting for the Viola

by Cassia Harvey

CHP258

©2014 C. Harvey Publications® All Rights Reserved.
www.charveypublications.com - print books & free sheet music blog
www.learnstrings.com - downloadable books & chamber music

C Major Shifting for the Viola
1
Cassia Harvey

©2014 C. Harvey Publications All Rights Reserved.

2

3

4

5

6

7

8

9

10

11

C Major Shifting for the Viola

12

13

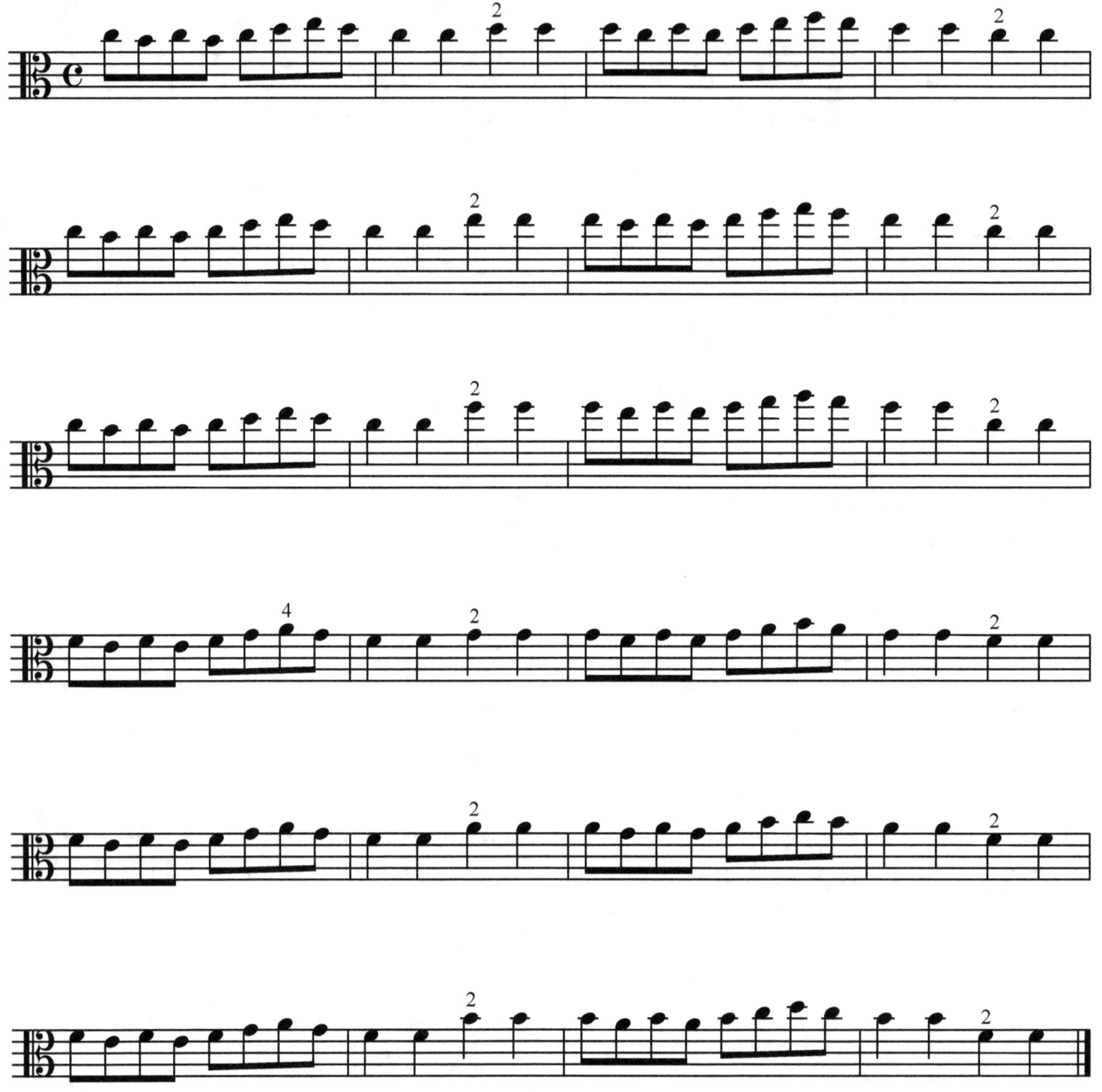

14

15

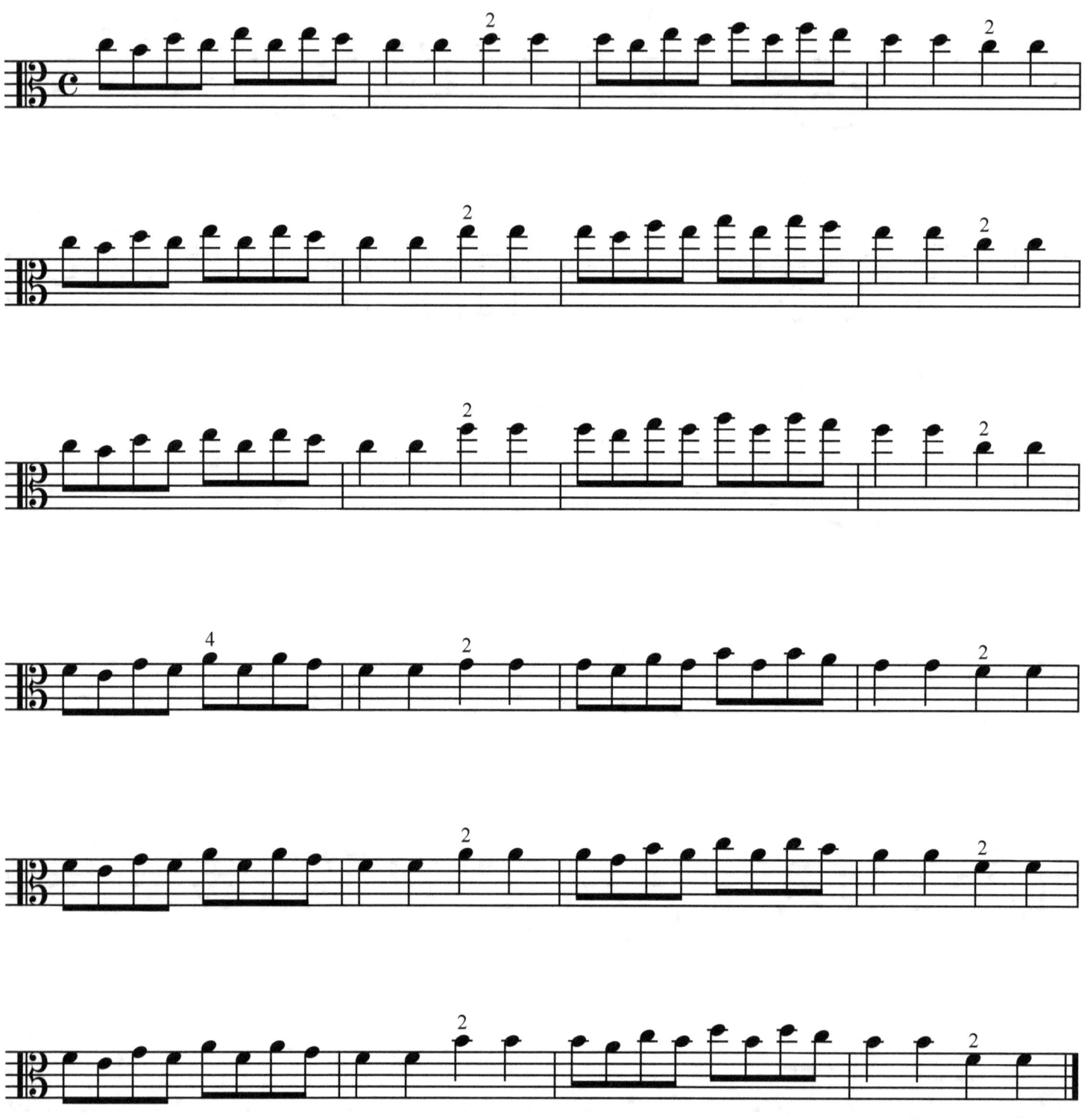

16

17

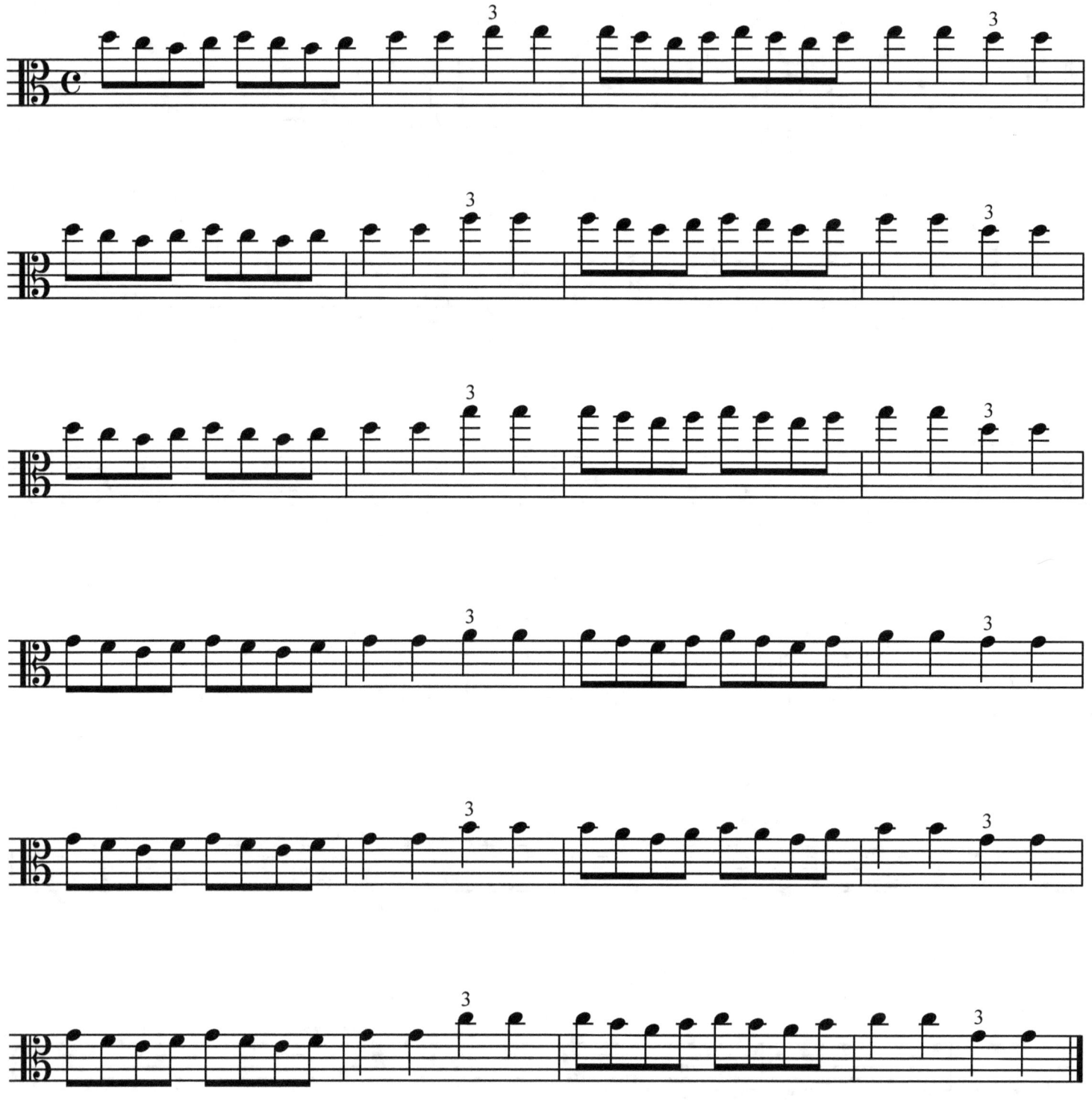

18

19

C Major Shifting for the Viola

20

21

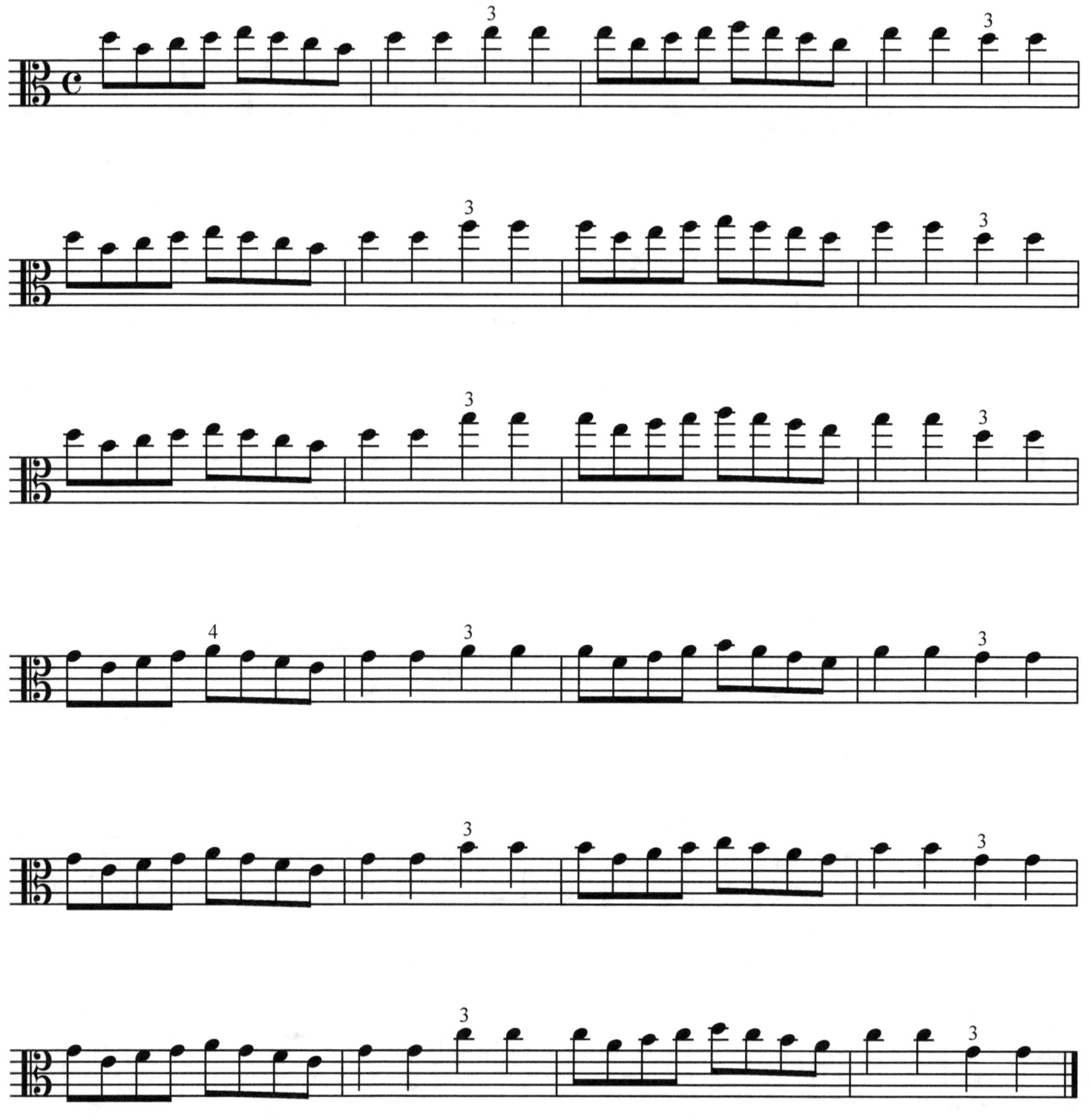

C Major Shifting for the Viola

22

23

24

25

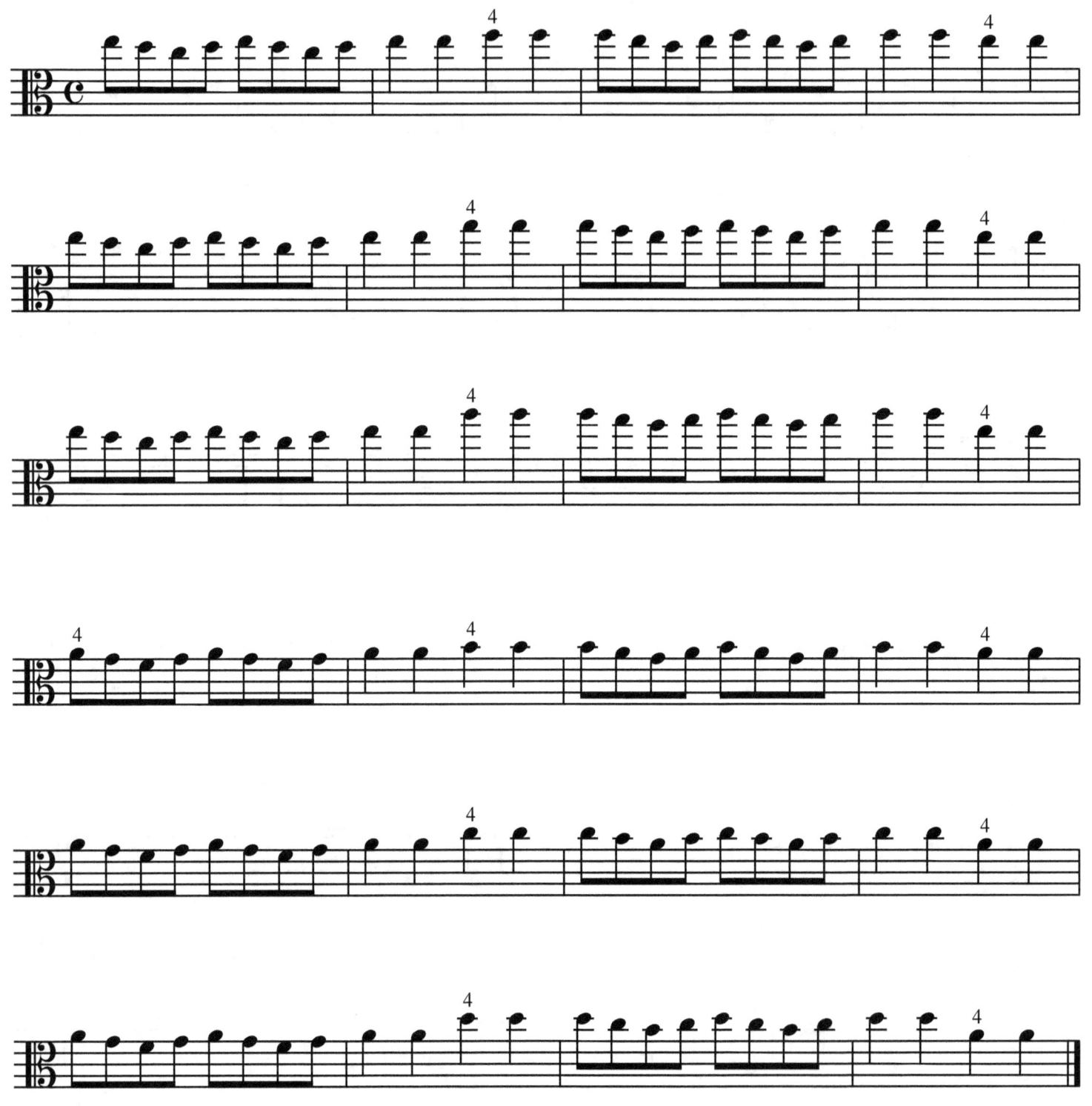

26

27

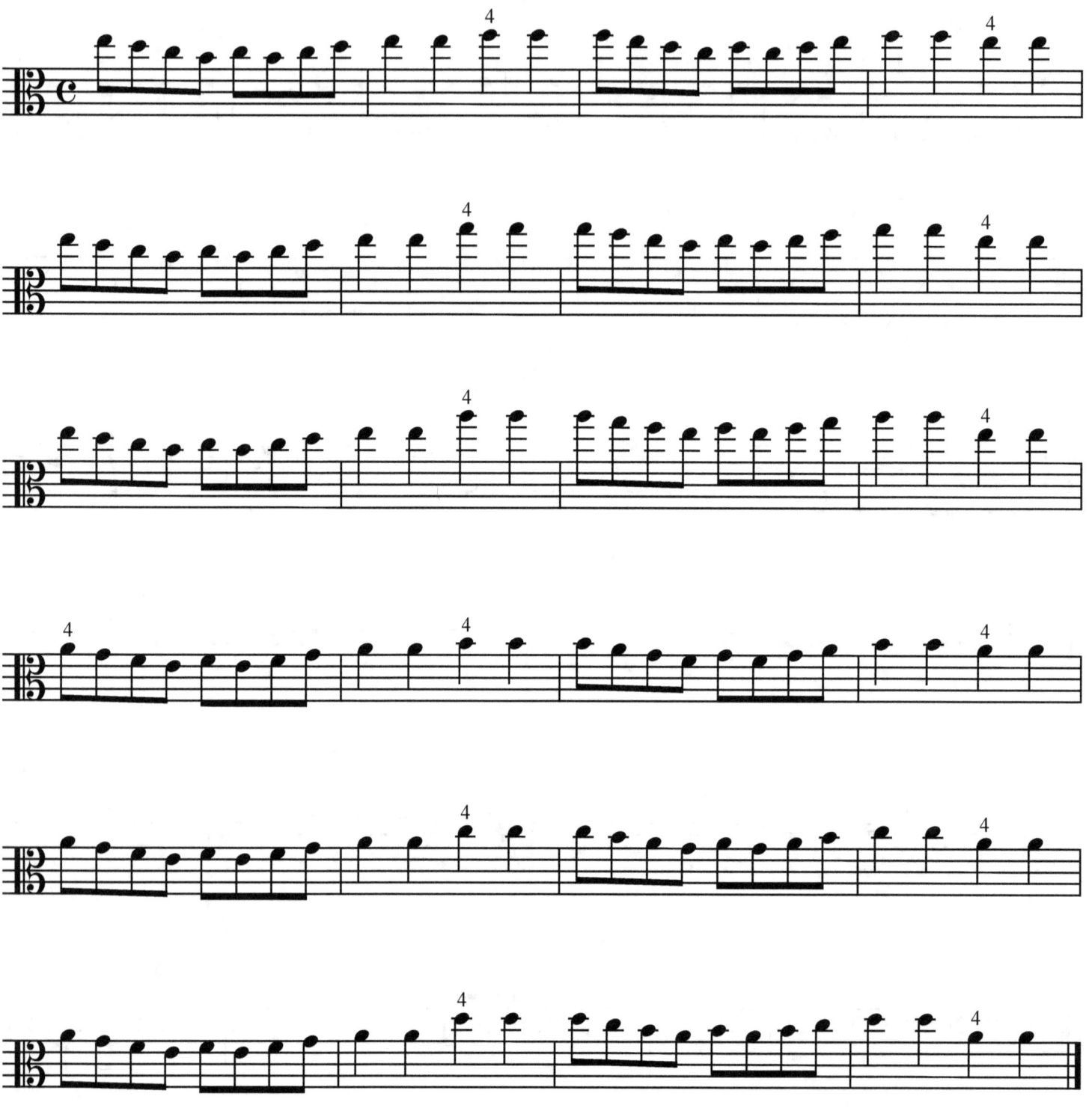

C Major Shifting for the Viola

28

29

30

31

C Major Shifting for the Viola

32

available from www.charveypublications.com: CHP203

Serial Shifting for the Viola

Cassia Harvey

©2012 C. Harvey Publications All Rights Reserved.